Ignite your Inner Flame

Tanya Joe

NAME :

DATE :

Notes

Welcome

Ignite Your Inner Flame is not just a journal – it's a journey.

A sanctuary for your deepest thoughts, unspoken truths, and untold stories. Through 100 thought-provoking questions, this journal invites you to confront your past, embrace your present, and ignite the fire of transformation within.

Write fearlessly. Reflect deeply. When you're ready, let the flames consume the pages – releasing what no longer serves you. This is your personal ritual of healing, growth, and renewal.

"Dare to burn the past and rise from the ashes."

DATE: / /

Self-Discovery & Identity

Self-Discovery & Identity explores the core of who you truly are. These themes challenge you to uncover your deepest values, hidden truths, and personal evolution. You'll reflect on the beliefs that shaped you, the moments that defined you, and the parts of yourself you may not always reveal. Through introspection, you'll gain clarity on your authentic self—who you were, who you are, and who you're becoming.

What are the three core values that define me?

DATE: / /

If I could describe myself in one sentence, what would it be?

What childhood dream did I give up on, and why?

DATE: / /

How have I changed in the past five years?

What is something I wish people knew about me but never say?

DATE: / /

What is the hardest truth I've ever had to accept about myself?

What part of myself do I hide from the world?

DATE: / /

What is a belief I once held strongly but have since abandoned?

Who am I when no one is watching?

DATE: / /

Memories & Reflection

Memories & Reflection delves into the moments that have shaped you—both the joyous and the painful. These themes guide you through your past, revisiting defining experiences, cherished memories, and pivotal turning points. By reflecting on where you've been, you gain deeper insight into how those moments continue to influence your present and future.

What is the happiest moment of my life so far?

DATE: / /

What is the saddest moment I've ever experienced?

Who from my past do I miss the most?

DATE: / /

What's a moment from childhood that shaped who I am?

What is a memory I wish I could erase?

DATE: / /

If I could send a letter to my younger self, what would it say?

What's the most embarrassing thing I've ever done?

DATE: / /

If I could relive one day, which would it be?

What moment in my life felt like a turning point?

DATE: / /

Inner Peace Exercise: The Pause Between Flames

Before continuing your journey, take a deep breath and pause. This moment is for you—to release tension, quiet the noise within, and embrace stillness.

Step 1: Breathe & Reset
Close your eyes and take five slow, deep breaths. With each inhale, welcome calm. With each exhale, let go of any lingering weight from your reflections.

Step 2: The Release List
On the notes page, write down three things that disturb your inner peace—fears, regrets, or negative thoughts. Acknowledge them, then whisper:
"You no longer control me. I set you free."

Step 3: The Affirmation Flame
Now, replace what you released with three affirmations of strength and peace. Examples:

- I am enough, just as I am.
- I choose growth over guilt.
- My past does not define me; my peace does.

Step 4: A Moment of Stillness
Sit in silence for a minute. Feel the space you've just created within yourself.
Now, turn the page and continue your journey—lighter, freer, at peace.

DATE: / /

Notes

DATE: / /

Notes

DATE: / /

Love & Relationships

Love & Relationships explores the connections that shape your heart—both the love you've given and received. These themes guide you through reflections on deep bonds, heartbreaks, unspoken words, and the lessons learned from relationships past and present. By examining love in all its forms—romantic, platonic, and self-love—you gain clarity on what truly matters in the connections you nurture.

What does love mean to me?

DATE: / /

What is the most heartbreaking goodbye I've ever said?

Who has hurt me the most, and have I forgiven them?

DATE: / /

What is one thing I've never said to someone I loved?

How do I show love to others?

DATE: / /

What is the greatest act of love I have ever witnessed?

What is a love story I will never forget?

DATE: / /

Who in my life do I trust completely?

Have I ever been in love, or just in love with the idea of it?

DATE: / /

Regrets & Forgiveness

Regrets & Forgiveness dives into the wounds of the past—the mistakes, missed chances, and words left unsaid. These themes encourage you to confront your regrets, acknowledge their lessons, and release the weight they carry. Through reflection, you'll explore the power of forgiveness—not just for others, but for yourself—allowing you to move forward with greater freedom and peace.

What is my biggest regret?

DATE: / /

If I could apologize to one person, who would it be and why?

What is something I need to forgive myself for?

DATE: / /

Have I ever sought revenge, and did it bring me peace?

What mistake do I keep repeating?

DATE: / /

Have I ever held onto a grudge for too long?

What is something I should have said, but never did?

DATE: / /

If today was my last day, would I be at peace?

What does forgiveness feel like to me?

DATE: / /

Inner Peace Exercise: Releasing the Past, Embracing the

After exploring love, loss, regrets, and forgiveness, take a moment to cleanse your heart and mind. This exercise will help you let go of emotional burdens and invite peace into your soul.

Step 1: Heart Check-In

Close your eyes and place a hand over your heart. Take three slow, deep breaths. Ask yourself:

- What emotions feel heavy right now?
- Is there love I need to accept or release?
- Is there a past wound I'm still carrying?

Step 2: The Letting Go Letter

On the notes page, write a short letter to someone (or yourself) expressing what you need to release. It can be an apology, a farewell, or simply an acknowledgment of pain. Example starters:

- Dear [Name], I forgive you for...
- To my past self, I want you to know...
- I am releasing the hurt of...

When finished, take a deep breath and say:
"I release this pain. It no longer belongs to me."

Step 3: A Mantra for Peace

Write a personal mantra to remind yourself of the love and forgiveness you choose to embrace. Example:

- I am worthy of love and healing.
- I forgive so I can be free.
- My heart is open, my soul is at peace.

DATE: / /

Exercise: Releasing the Past, Embracing the Heart

Step 4: A Moment of Stillness

Close your eyes for one minute. Visualize yourself lighter, unburdened, and free. When ready, turn the page and continue with a peaceful heart.

DATE: / /

Notes

DATE: / /

Notes

DATE: / /

Fear & Darkness

Fear & Darkness uncovers the shadows within—the fears, insecurities, and hidden thoughts we often avoid. These themes challenge you to face your deepest anxieties, confront past betrayals, and acknowledge the moments you felt lost or alone. By shining a light on the darkness, you reclaim your power, turning fear into strength and pain into growth.

What am I most afraid of?

DATE: / /

What is my deepest insecurity?

What is a nightmare that has stayed with me?

DATE: / /

Have I ever betrayed someone?

Do I believe in karma?

DATE: / /

What is the worst thing I have ever done?

Have I ever faced my fears head-on?

DATE: / /

If my darkest thoughts had a voice, what would they say?

Have I ever faced my fears head-on?

DATE: / /

Dreams & Desires

Dreams & Desires explores the deepest longings of your heart—the ambitions, passions, and unspoken wishes that drive you. These themes help you uncover what truly excites and fulfills you, whether it's a lifelong goal or a hidden desire you've yet to pursue. By reflecting on your dreams, you gain clarity on what you want from life and the steps needed to turn aspirations into reality.

What is my ultimate dream in life?

DATE: / /

What does happiness look like to me?

What is something I secretly desire but never admit?

DATE: / /

If I could start over anywhere in the world, where would it be?

What do I crave the most in life?

DATE: / /

Have I settled for less than I deserve?

What is my personal definition of success?

DATE: / /

If I had unlimited money, what would I do first?

What is my dream version of myself?

DATE: / /

Inner Peace Exercise: Embracing After the Shadows

After diving into your dreams, desires, fears, and darkness, take this moment to cleanse your spirit and realign with your inner peace.

Step 1: The Breath of Renewal

Close your eyes and take a deep inhale. Hold it for a moment, then slowly exhale. Imagine breathing out fear and doubt, and inhaling clarity and courage. Repeat this three times.

Step 2: Transforming Fear into Strength

On the notes page, write down one fear or insecurity that has been holding you back. Now, rewrite it as a strength.

- I fear failure Every setback is a lesson that makes me stronger.
- I fear being alone I am learning to love and trust myself.

Once finished, whisper:
"I reclaim my power. Fear does not define me."

Step 3: A Vision of Light

Close your eyes and picture yourself achieving one of your biggest dreams. Where are you? How do you feel? What do you see? Let this vision fill you with excitement and purpose. Now, write a single sentence that captures that feeling. Example:

- I am walking boldly toward my destiny.
- I am limitless, fearless, and unstoppable.
- My dreams are already becoming reality.

DATE: / /

Inner Peace Exercise: Embracing Light After the Shadows

Step 4: Grounding in Gratitude
Write down three things you are grateful for in this moment. Gratitude anchors you in peace and reminds you of the light that already exists in your life.

Step 5: A Moment of Stillness
Close your eyes once more, feeling lighter, braver, and ready to move forward. When you're ready, turn the page and continue your journey —stronger than before.

DATE: / /

Notes

DATE: / /

Notes

DATE: / /

Letting Go & Moving On

Letting Go & Moving On is about releasing the past and making space for new beginnings. These themes guide you through recognizing what no longer serves you—old wounds, past relationships, regrets, or limiting beliefs. By acknowledging, accepting, and letting go, you free yourself from emotional weight, allowing healing, growth, and a renewed sense of peace to take root.

What is something I need to release from my life?

DATE: / /

Have I ever held onto something that was destroying me?

What is the hardest lesson life has taught me?

DATE: / /

How do I handle change?

What chapter of my life needs to close?

DATE: / /

Who or what do I need to let go of?

How do I want to be remembered?

DATE: / /

What words would I put on my own tombstone?

What final message do I have for my past self?

DATE: / /

The Unknown & Mystical

The Unknown & Mystical explores the mysteries of life—fate, destiny, the afterlife, and the unexplainable. These themes invite you to question, wonder, and reflect on the forces beyond our understanding. Whether it's intuition, synchronicities, or the unknown paths ahead, this section encourages you to embrace the magic of uncertainty and find meaning in life's unanswered questions.

Do I believe in fate, or do I make my own destiny?

DATE: / /

If I could speak to my future self, what would I ask?

Do I believe in life after death?

DATE: / /

If ghosts exist, what would mine say about me?

Have I ever experienced something unexplainable?

DATE: / /

What is the closest I've come to death?

If I could ask the universe one question, what would it be?

DATE: / /

Do I believe in soulmates?

What does my intuition tell me that my logic ignores?

DATE: / /

Inner Peace Exercise: Surrendering to the Flow of Life

After exploring the mysteries of the unknown and the power of letting go, take this moment to embrace trust, release control, and find peace in uncertainty.

Step 1: Deep Breath & Trust
Close your eyes and take a deep breath in. As you inhale, imagine drawing in trust and acceptance. As you exhale, let go of the need for control. Repeat three times.

Step 2: Writing to the Universe
On the notes page, write a letter to the universe (or a higher power, fate, or your future self). Express your hopes, fears, and dreams. End with the words:
"I surrender to the journey. I trust where life is taking me."

Step 3: The Ritual of Release
Write down one thing you still struggle to let go of. Now, beneath it, write:
"I release this with love. I am free."
Tear out the page, crumple it, or safely burn it as a symbol of surrender.

Step 4: Affirmation of Peace
Replace what you've released with an affirmation:

- I trust the timing of my life.
- I am safe in the unknown.
- Letting go brings me peace.

DATE: / /

Inner Peace Exercise: Surrendering to the Flow of Life

Step 5: A Moment of Stillness

Close your eyes, place a hand over your heart, and sit in silence for one minute. Feel the weight lift. Feel yourself becoming lighter. When you're ready, turn the page and move forward—open, free, and at peace.

DATE: / /

Notes

DATE: / /

Notes

DATE: / /

Self-Worth & Growth

Self-Worth & Growth is about recognizing your value and embracing personal evolution. These themes encourage deep reflection on your strengths, achievements, and the lessons learned through challenges. By acknowledging your growth and self-worth, you cultivate confidence, resilience, and the belief that you are enough—just as you are, while still becoming who you're meant to be.

Do I truly love myself?

DATE: / /

What is something I've overcome that I never thought I would?

How have I surprised myself?

DATE: / /

What is a weakness that I have turned into strength?

How do I define self-worth?

DATE: / /

What would I tell someone struggling with what I've been through?

What habits are holding me back?

DATE: / /

Have I ever betrayed myself to please others?

What is my personal mantra?

DATE: / /

Final Thoughts - Self Renewal

Final Thoughts - Self Renewal is a moment of reflection before self-release. These themes encourage you to revisit your journey, acknowledge your growth, and honor the emotions, memories, and lessons within these pages. It's a space to express gratitude, set intentions, and prepare for the symbolic act of letting go —turning the past into ashes and stepping into a renewed sense of self.

If this journal is my confessional, what sins do I need to let go of?

DATE: / /

What is something that still haunts me?

If this journal is a letter to the universe, what is my request?

DATE: / /

What is the heaviest burden I carry?

What is the secret I will never tell anyone?

DATE: / /

What is my final goodbye to the past?

If I could rewrite my story, what would the new ending be?

DATE: / /

What lesson do I take with me after completing this journal?

Who do I become?

DATE: / /

Inner Peace Exercise: Embracing Your

As you reach the final stages of this journal journey, take this moment to honor your growth, recognize your worth, and step into a new chapter with peace and confidence.

Step 1: Deep Breath & Acknowledgment
Close your eyes and take a slow, deep breath. As you inhale, welcome self-acceptance. As you exhale, release any lingering self-doubt. Repeat three times.

Step 2: Letter to Your Future Self
On the notes page, write a letter to your future self. Reflect on how far you've come and where you hope to go. Offer yourself encouragement, wisdom, and a reminder that you are strong, worthy, and always evolving.

Step 3: The Power Statement
Write one sentence that defines your transformation. Example:

- I am at peace with my past and excited for my future.
- I have released what no longer serves me, and I am free.
- I am strong, worthy, and ready for whatever comes next.

Step 4: A Moment of Gratitude
List three things you are grateful for about yourself—your strength, resilience, kindness, or growth.

DATE: / /

Inner Peace Exercise: Embracing Your New Beginning

Step 5: Silence & Renewal

Close your eyes for a full minute. Feel the weight of the past lift, making space for the new. When you're ready, turn the page—lighter, stronger, and at peace.

DATE: / /

Notes

DATE: / /

Notes

DATE: / /

Closing Pages of Ignite Your Inner Flame

A Final Moment of Reflection

As you close this journal, take a deep breath and acknowledge the journey you've taken within these pages. Every word you wrote, every emotion you explored, and every truth you uncovered has brought you closer to yourself. You have faced your past, embraced your present, and ignited the fire for your future.

The Ritual of Release

If you choose to, you may now complete the final step—letting go. Whether you burn these pages, tear them apart, or simply close this book and tuck it away, know that the act of release is yours to define. However you choose to move forward, trust that you are lighter, freer, and ready for what's next.

Final Thoughts

Before you say goodbye to these pages, take a moment to write a closing statement—one last thought, intention, or affirmation. Example:

What do you want to carry forward from this experience?

How do you feel in this moment?

What message would you leave for your future self?

DATE: / /

A Note to You

No matter what you've released, what you've discovered, or what still remains unanswered—know that you are enough. You are strong, worthy, and capable of transformation. Your past does not define you. Your future is unwritten. And most importantly...

You are free...

Now, step forward. The fire within you burns brighter than ever.

A Heartfelt Thank You

To you, the brave soul who embarked on this journey—thank you. Thank you for showing up for yourself, for daring to face your truth, and for embracing the power of reflection and release. Within these pages, you have poured your heart out, confronted your past, and ignited the fire within. That takes courage. That takes strength. And that is something to be proud of.

Whether you choose to keep these words or let them go in the flames, know that this journey was never about the pages—it was always about you. Your growth. Your healing. Your transformation.

May you move forward lighter, freer, and more in tune with the person you are meant to be. The past is ashes, the future is unwritten, and you are limitless.

With gratitude and light,

-**Tanya Joe**

Notes

Notes

Notes

.. End of Journal ..

www.ingramcontent.com/pod-product-compliance
Lightning Source LLC
LaVergne TN
LVHW070942160826
845679LV00022B/1885

9798897444779